Beginnings and Endings

Kate Cobb and Michèle Barca

HRD PRESS
Amherst, Massachusetts

In association with
Connaught Training

Published in North America by *HRD Press*
22 Amherst Road
Amherst, Massachusetts 01002

In association with CONNAUGHT training

ISBN 0-87425-249-0

Production Services by Jack Sanders
Cover Design by Old Mill Graphics

CONTENTS

PART ONE: Beginnings

Introduction

The purpose of this manual is to provide a set of activities to use either at the beginning or at the end of a training course. Whether or not you are new to this type of activity, there will be a variety from which to choose.

If you already use these activities, then you will appreciate their value in the formation, development and effectiveness of your training. When appropriately used, they can increase the cohesiveness of the group of participants and create a relaxed atmosphere, thus enhancing the learning experience. You will find that the level of group participation rises in response to such activities.

So why doesn't every trainer use them all the time? Obviously you need to use such exercises—ice breakers, energizers, etc—appropriately and sparingly; you *can* have too much of a good thing! More often reluctance to participate comes, from the trainers themselves not from the group. Sometimes you may not be particularly alert at the beginning of a course; you may not be in the mood to be a fruit (see Activity 13); you may be tired at the end of a program and just want the group to leave so that you can pack up and go home. Trainers are human beings, however. No doubt we've all felt this way sometimes and if you can raise enough enthusiasm for the activity, you will find that your energy also rises and the benefits to all will be enormous.

Sometimes our own feelings about ourselves and our roles prevent us from using a particular activity. Some trainers may find it uncomfortable miming their hobbies (see Activity 17) in front of a group of strangers. In that case, don't use that type of activity: If you force yourself to, your own embarrassment will show through to the group and the activity may fail. The activities in this manual were designed for all trainers, from the most reserved to the most extroverted, so choose what you are comfortable with. Once you see the results, you will become confident enough to take more risks.

There's no point pretending that using such activities doesn't involve risks on your part; it does, and you may find that no one wants to join in. But this is highly unlikely if you have the right amount of enthusiasm and commitment, as you would do with any other training activity. The reason for this is clear, especially at the beginning of a course when people are probably feeling anxious and uncertain. Generally, they do not want to see the trainer fail because in terms of the dynamics of the group, you are the leader (whether you like this or not). Challenges to your leadership may arise from group members. This can be healthy or destructive depending on the way they are handled but, even so, you provide security for the group as leader and normally no one wants to see you fail. People will therefore support you by participating in your activities, even if they need a little encouragement at the beginning. If anyone still refuses to join in, they shouldn't be forced into participating. Be careful not to express any negative feelings you may have about them (it's natural in these circumstances to be a little angry with those who do not wish to join in with your carefully planned exercises). Try to find them another role in the activity—perhaps as observer or timekeeper—so that they are still involved.

This brings us to another important point. Normally you should explain the purpose of the exercise before you start (there *will* be occasions when doing this destroys the impact) and tell the groups what is going to happen with a particular drawing they've done or information they've revealed. (In other words, tell them how these will be used.) If, for example, participants don't know whether their fantasies (see Avtivity 24) are going to be revealed to the whole group or just their partner, this will increase their anxiety and, as a consequence, their level of hostility to the exercise (and you!) and reduce their level of participation.

As with everything you do as a trainer, you need to be sensitive to your group as a whole and to the individuals in that group. That means being aware of how your exercises may affect people on the basis of their class, color, age, gender, sexual orientation, disability, size and so on. This may seem obvious but when planning exercises be careful that you don't choose (or invent) something that could exclude a member of your group. For instance, if you give examples of names in an activity and you can see that you have cultural diversity, keep that in mind. This is equally true when working with a mixed race or gender group. If you are giving examples of hobbies to a group of women, don't restrict your choice to traditional women's activities, such as cooking and sewing ; you may very well have a woodworker in your midst. Maintain a wide perspective!
Be sensitive to any members of your group who have a disability and adapt exercises to suit them where possible. If you can't adapt a particular exercise, choose another exercise instead. Don't assume that you can judge a person's capabilities. If you have doubts about a particular exercise, find out ahead of time, whenever possible, who your participants are.

You may or may not consider it appropriate to join in some of the activities suggested in this book. Sometimes it is appropriate and useful but often it isn't. Beware of using the opportunity to discuss too much about yourself inappropriately with the group. In each activity it is made clear whether it is useful to join in or not, but ultimately you must decide for yourself. So remember:

1. Choose appropriate activities for your desired objective.
2. Don't expect participants to do things you wouldn't do.
3. Be clear about the purpose and outcome of each activity.
4. Be sensitive to individual differences.
5. It's worth taking risks!

Using this Manual

This manual contains seventy exercises that have been used by us during our years as trainers. We hope you will find them useful. They are classified as either "Beginnings" or "Endings." Each exercise includes an objective and in some cases, the type of group that the exercise is <u>particularly</u> suited for.

You will be able to see at a glance what materials you will need and how much time to allocate, although this is obviously only a guide and you may find that you take less or more time than we suggest.

All the exercises in this manual are based on a group of twelve people but can be adapted to larger or smaller groups. The type of room and amount of space should be appropriate to the activity, as well as the need for chairs.

The Method section contains your instructions as the trainer and, in some cases, a Trainer Guidance section to serve as a guide as to what you might say to your group about the exercise.

Where we know of other variations from the basic exercise, we have given them to you and under the Possible Pitfalls section we describe dangers to watch out for.

There is space at the end for you to make your own notes, should you wish to, about how the exercises have gone, what changes you might like to make, etc.

The looseleaf format will make it easy to extract each exercise as you need it.

We hope that you will try many of these exercises and that they add energy and fun to your training as well as providing a learning experience.

Index to the Activities
Beginnings

While all of these exercises are useful at the beginning of training sessions, some have a specific objective. The activities that are marked with an asterisk (*) have optional ending exercises to use with the same group.

Index to the Activities
Beginnings

Index to the Activities
Endings

While all of these exercises are useful at the end of training sessions, some have a specific objective in mind.

Activity	Page Number	Action Planning	Evaluation/Feedback of Course	Giving/Gaining Positive Feedback	Ongoing/Incremental Training	Ongoing Support	Personal Development
Letter to Myself	115	●					
Import-Export Game	111						
How Do I Feel Now?	109						●
Group Sound	107				●		
Group Shield	105		●	●	●		
Gift to the Group	103			●	●		
Gallery of Wants and Offers	101					●	
Different Ways to Say Goodbye	97				●		
Compliments	95			●			●
Color This Group	93			●	●		
Closing Circles	91		●				
Card To Remember Me By	89			●			
And Now Goodbye	87				●		
Action!	85	●					

Index to the Activities
Endings

While all of these exercises are useful at the end of training sessions, some have a specific objective in mind.

PART ONE:
Beginnings

How you open a session is crucial, it may not make or break a course (though sometimes it comes close!) but it can certainly save much time and energy later.

A training course starts as soon as you or the participants, whoever is first, enter the room and the process of creating rapport with your group begins then. You can set the tone you want by the way you greet people, make them welcome, help them feel comfortable and so on. The way you arrange the physical environment communicates much about the tone of the event to participants: Are they to sit behind desks and thus expect a teacher-led formal course or sit in a circle, with the trainer, in a more informal configuration.

The importance of creating rapport i.e. getting on the same wavelength as the group, cannot be over-emphasized: It means that right from the start the group will be with you and thus open and enthusiastic to learning. This doesn't mean that they won't have fears and anxieties but a relaxed atmosphere should encourage a sense of safety and security.

You will see that many of the Beginning exercises start with: "Ask participants to sit in a circle . . . . We believe that the most effective way to run training courses is informally, so people don't feel they are back at school but rather are equal to, and not inferior to the trainer. Even if we are conducting courses on writing skills, we still have people sitting in a circle for discussions. Tables for writing exercises are available when needed."

However, your style may be different, and so try to develop ways of working with which you are comfortable. Bear in mind, though, that physical barriers create psychological barriers, so, have the confidence to eliminate them where possible.

We have already created an atmosphere with our group before we have even begun the course. Why, then, bother with a Beginning exercise? The reasons include:

1. to provide a shared experience for the whole group, which helps to build cohesiveness and trust;

2. to focus people's attention on the course and away from their other preoccupations;

3. to continue the rapport-creating process;

4. to learn and remember people's names so that no one has to resort to badges or name tags (which depersonalizes the training process and rather defeats the objective);

5. to extract any particular learning point pertinent to the topic of the course;

6. to raise the energy level and prepare for learning; and

7. to have fun! (but not at the group's or an individual's expense).

As with any training exercises, activities should be selected that are relevant and appropriate to your group and to your objectives. Be careful not to choose something too challenging for a group of people new to each other, and do not expect them to reveal too much about themselves until you have created the right atmosphere for this to happen. Always be sensitive to the baggage people bring to training courses, that is, the experiences and feelings of their entire life (not just work) that they are carrying around with them. They may or may not reveal any of these things and certainly no one will reveal anything until a proper (safe) environment is created with you and the group. Certain activities may bring unpleasant memories to the fore, e.g. a participant may have recently suffered a bereavement, or be very unhappy in a job, or have had an argument with a co-worker that morning. If anyone does express particularly heightened emotions, either anger or tears, then deal with it sensitively and try not to be embarrassed or defensive.

Choosing a beginning exercise that starts the course well can improve the way the group responds to your other learning activities and to the training as a whole.

1
Alphabet Game

Objective

This activity is an energizer that demonstrates the concept of synergy in a group. It is useful in team building.

Materials

- Flipchart paper and pen.
- A text to read from.
- Paper for participants to write on.

Time

30 minutes.

Method

1. Write the letters of the alphabet A-Z down the left-hand side of a piece of flipchart paper, one under another.

2. Ask participants to write this in the same way on their paper.

3. Choose a sentence or two (which has 26 letters) from any text and next to each letter of the alphabet write a second letter taken from your text so you end up with 26 pairs of letters, e.g. AT, BH, CE, DC, EA, FT (The text chosen here is "the cat sat on the mat"). Read these letters aloud as you are writing them so that participants can also add them to their first list.

4. Explain that these pairs of letters could be the initials of famous people, living or dead, real or fictional, and they have to think of as many names as they can of people with these initials in 5 minutes and write them down.

5. Give them the time to do this and then ask them to exchange their list with someone else in the group. Their partners will now review the list and agree or disagree with the names written down, i.e. that they are in fact famous people. If they agree, then their partner scores one point; if they disagree, then their partner has to try to convince them that they are right. If they can convince them, they score another point but if they cannot they have to cross that name out and score nothing. Allow enough time (about 5 minutes) for both people to look at each other's lists.

6. Go around the group and make a note of the scores of each person.

7. Divide the group into subgroups (about six maximum) and ask each group again to repeat the process of finding names of famous people using the same letters. They can offer the names they have already thought of individually or find new ones; it doesn't matter. Give them the same time (5 minutes) and a sheet of flipchart paper to prepare their list.

8. While they are doing this, you can find the average by adding together all the individual scores and dividing by the number of people in the group.

9. At the end of the time, each group presents their list. The trainer challenges if there is only one group. And the other group(s) has the right to challenge as before.

10. Look at the score(s) for each subgroup and use the average from step 8 above. On almost every occasion you will find that the scores achieved by people working together in groups are greater than that achieved by each individual.

11. This can lead to a discussion or further exercises about the importance of effective teamwork.

In the very unlikely event that you arrive at a group score that is smaller than the individual average, you will need to explain what usually happens.

Notes

2

Animals

Objective

The purpose of this activity is to introduce each other and share some information about each other with the group. It is most useful for personal development training or for an ongoing group.

Materials

None.

Time

30 minutes.

Method

1. Ask participants to think of an animal they would like to be, e.g. lion, rabbit.

2. Ask participants one at a time to say their name and their animal, e.g. "I am Michele the antelope" and then to speak as this animal, saying what they like and don't like about being that animal. (Strengths and weaknesses).

3. Go around so that everyone has a turn.

4. When everyone has spoken, ask participants to pair up with someone else in the group and to share with their partner why they chose that animal and whether there are any similarities with their life in the strengths and weaknesses they spoke of and whether they want to achieve any of the qualities that the animal possesses. Allow 10 minutes for this stage.

5. After 10 minutes, ask the participants to come back into a circle and ask for general feedback of anything significant anyone wants to share from their discussions. Don't force anyone to reveal anything they don't want to.

Variations

1. Ask participants to draw the animal and "wear" the drawing while they introduce themselves.

2. Use any other class of things, e.g. plants, cars, furniture.

Possible Pitfalls

Some people may disclose very personal thoughts, e.g. they might realize they have certain qualities lacking in their lives, so you need to be supportive and sensitive to this.

Notes

3
Apples and Pears

Objective

The purpose of this acitvity, suitable for any group to learn what expectations people have and what they hope to gain from the training program, as well as any concerns they might have.

Materials

*   2 sheets of flipchart paper.
*   Flipchart pens.

Time

20 to 30 minutes.

Method

1. Explain what you are going to do (see Trainer Guidance) and ask participants to think about their expectations and possible concerns about the course. These should be hopes and fears about the course itself rather than any possible outcomes or work issues related to the topic.

2. While they are doing this, draw a very large tree on each piece of flipchart paper and, on one sheet, draw apple shapes inside the tree for expectations; on the other draw pear shapes inside the tree for fears and concerns regarding the course. There should be enough apples and pears for each person to write something in each and these should be large enough for people to write a few words inside. (You may prefer to prepare this before the start of the course.)

3. Ask people to come to the board, one at a time and explain their expectations and concerns, if any, about the course and then to write a word or short phrase summarizing this inside either the apple or the pear as appropriate.

4. Once everyone has spoken, go through the expectations sheet with the group, pointing out what will and will not be covered by the course.

5. Then go through the concerns sheet, reassuring people (if appropriate) about the content and method of the course.

6. These sheets can then be displayed until the end of the program and reviewed with the group as part of your evaluation of the course.

Trainer Guidance

An explanation of the course may be along the following lines: "We're going to be together for [x] days and it would be useful to know just what you expect to gain from this course and any fears you may have about being here. I'd like you to think for a few minutes about what your expectations are of this training program and any concerns you may have about it and then to come up and tell us what they are. I'd then like you to write a word or short phrase that sums up what you feel in either an apple for expectations or a pear for concerns. You may not have any fears about being here of course, but I hope you have some expectations."

Variation

Ask people to pair up at the beginning and have each person spend 5 minutes verbalizing expectations and fears to each other before they tell the rest of the group.

Possible Pitfalls

Any exercise that seeks to elicit expectations from a group can run into problems if, for example, someone has been sent on a course and is clearly resentful about being there. If this comes up, you need to treat it sensitively and explore the person's feelings a little at that stage and maybe (depending on the objective and the norms of your organization) give the person the option to withdraw. Participants may also express other "negative" feelings about being there and it is as well to know these early on and deal with them at the beginning. If you don't they may well emerge in other ways later on and could result in sabotaging your whole program.

Notes

4
Back to Back

Objective

The purpose of this activity is for paticipants to become aware of the importance of both verbal and nonverbal feedback in communication. This activity is suitable for any training on communication skills.

Materials

None.

Time

20 minutes.

Method

1. Ask participants to pair up, preferably with someone they don't know. (If you don't have even numbers in the group, you may decide to join in yourself). The exercise is rather difficult to do with an odd number.

2. Ask them to decide who is going to be A and who is B (i.e. who's going first and second).

3. Ask each pair to place their chairs back to back so that they can't see each other. Tell them to spread out as much as possible to avoid being distracted by other pairs.

4. Ask A's to speak to B's for 3 minutes. They should introduce themselves during that time, telling where they work and something about themselves such as interests and hobbies.

5. At the end of 3 minutes, B's should briefly verify what they heard with A's so that they will be able to introduce them later.

6. The B's then speak to A's for 3 minutes. The B's check what they heard from A's and the groups return to a large circle.

7. Each person introduces his/her partner to the rest of the group.

8. When all introductions are completed, ask participants what it was like to be (a) a speaker and (b) a listener.

You can draw many learning points from the difficulties most people encounter in listening attentively when they cannot see the other person.

Variation

Participants can specifically be asked to talk about their expectations of the course rather than hobbies and you can write these on the flipchart during the feedback.

Notes

5

Behind My Back

Objective

The purpose of this activity, suitable for any group, is to introduce the group and gain insight into how other people see you.

Materials

- Flipchart paper and pens.
- Some type of adhesive tape.

Time

30 minutes.

Method

1. Introduce the activity (see Trainer Guidance).

2. Ask each person to take a piece of flipchart paper and write his/her name at the top and then ask someone else to tape it on their back.

3. Ask the group to mingle and, when they encounter someone, write something about that person on his/her "back."

4. After everyone has written on everyone else (allow about 15 to 20 minutes) ask the group to take off the sheets and sit in a circle.

5. Give them time to read the comments others have made and to make any comments they want to the group about the exercise.

6. Ask each person to choose one of the statements that has pleased them most or is most significant to them and then go around asking everyone to introduce themselves with their name and to read aloud the statement from their own point of view e.g. "My name is Doug and I look confident."

Trainer Guidance

You can introduce the activity along the following lines: "This is a useful exercise about first impressions and how others see you. I'd like you to think about the people you see in this group and what positive first impressions you have about them. They may look very confident or full of fun or you may feel you'd like to get to know them."

Notes

6

Book Jacket

Objective

The purpose of this activity, suitable for any group, is to practice introductions in a group.

Material

- Paper and pens.
- Some type of adhesive tape (optional).

Time

30 minutes.

Method

1. Ask participants to imagine they have written a book that is about to be published. They have to write a short piece about themselves (not more than 50 words) that will appear on the book jacket under the title "About the Author." Allow up to 10 minutes for this.

2. Ask each person to read aloud his/her description to the rest of the group.

They need to include their name and they may want to say something about where they live or their family or achievements in life, whatever they think is significant.

Variation

Ask participants to write their descriptions on flipchart paper and post them on the walls until the end of the course. They then may like to add or amend the piece in some way.

Notes

7

Breathing Through Your Toes

Objective

The purpose of this activity is to help participants relax before beginning a training activity. It is particularly useful for stress management and personal awareness groups.

Materials

None.

Time

20 to 30 minutes.

Method

1. Offer participants the option of sitting or lying on the floor for this exercise, whatever they find most comfortable.

2. Introduce the activity along the following lines: "Once you are really comfortable, I'd like you to imagine that your toes are nostrils and that each time you breathe in the air goes in through your toes, moves slowly through your body and goes out through your nose. Imagine that as you breath out, each muscle of your whole body becomes very relaxed. Again breathe in through your toes and out through your nose.

   "Now I would like you to recall a wonderful time that you had, perhaps a vacation, and enjoy looking at it again in your mind's eye. I will give you a few minutes to regain the feeling of that experience [Allow silence for 2—3 minutes].

"Now gently open your eyes and return your attention to the room and to the training. How do you feel?"

3. Ask them to close their eyes, and deliver, distinctly but slowly, the instructions for this exercise.

4. Once you have completed the exercise, allow a few seconds for people to come back to full awareness and ask them how they are feeling.

Possible Pitfalls

Sometimes when people are really relaxed they become tearful so be prepared to be supportive at first, and then help any affected participant to return to the task at hand.

Notes

8
Bunny Game

Objectives

The purpose of this activity, suitable for any group, is to learn people's names.

Materials

A soft toy such as a stuffed animal.

Time

15 minutes.

Method

1. Ask the group to stand in a circle and explain the purpose of the activity.

2. Go around the group twice asking each person, in turn, to say his/her name.

3. Explain that you are going to throw the toy at someone and say his/her name and if you get it right that person then throws it to someone else saying his/her name and so on.

4. If a participant can't remember someone's name or mispronounces it then the person catching the toy throws the toy back to the participant, saying it correctly.

5. They will then throw it on to someone else and once everyone understands the game, you can begin to speed up for more fun!

6. Finish when you feel everyone knows everyone else's name.

Variation

You can use this purely as a reminder of people's names once participants have already introduced themselves in some way. In this case you would omit step 2 in the Method above.

Possible Pitfalls

If you have wheel-chair users in your group, you can play this game sitting down. (Obviously, this would not be a suitable activity if anyone has a particular disability with their hands or arms.)

Notes

9

Creating Rapport

Objective

The purpose of this activity is for participants to become better acquainted. This is particularly useful for any awareness training.

Materials

None.

Time

30 minutes.

Method

1. Ask the group to form pairs (or a three if necessary).

2. Ask them to decide who is A and who is B (or C if there is a three).

3. A is going to mirror B, i.e. adopt the same posture, the way they are sitting, position of the head, hand/foot movements, etc., while talking with B about a topic of interest for 5 minutes.

4. After 5 minutes ask for feedback from A about what it was like to be B and any comments from B.

5. Exchange roles so that B now mirrors A for 5 minutes and take feedback as before.

[C acts as an observer and gives feedback in their small group. You can allow more time so that C also has a chance of mirroring in the group of three.]

6. Return to the large group and ask for general comments.

Notes

10
Deliveries

Objectives

The purpose of this activity, suitable for any group, is to gain an idea of people's expectations and what may be issues for them.

Materials

- Flipchart and pen.

Time

30 minutes.

Method

1. Explain that training is like going on a journey (see Trainer Guidance). Ask each person to spend 5 minutes thinking for themselves and writing down what they hope to learn on this journey (i.e. expectations) and what they are hoping to "deliver" (i.e. dispose of, contribute to the group and so on).

2. Ask participants to introduce themselves, one at a time, and explain what they have learned and what they will deliver.

3. You could write on a flipchart what is said on two separate sheets.

Trainer Guidance

A brief explanation of the above analogy can be given along the following lines: "I would like you to consider for a moment that we are going on a journey. Training is always a bit like a journey as you may be going down a new route, hoping to discover new things or perhaps going over ground you've traveled before but this time wanting to see more than just the main road.

"What I'd like you to do is to consider for about 5 minutes what you are hoping to acquire on this journey and what you are hoping to distribute - in other words what do you want to gain from the course, what do you want to change about yourself and what can you contribute to the rest of the group? It may help to write these things down."

Notes

11
Dings and Dongs

Objective

This activity, suitable for any group, is a useful and enjoyable energizer for any group.

Materials

Two small objects that can be easily handled and passed around, e.g. a ball, different colored flipchart pens.

Time

20 minutes.

Method

1. Decide on two objects that you are going to use.

2. Ask everyone to form a circle with their chairs fairly close together.

3. Explain what you want them to do (see Trainer Guidance but don't spend too much time on explanations. This game is much easier to play than to describe.

4. Ask the person on your left if he/she will help you pass the "dong" around around so that this person is the starting and finishing point for this exercise.

5. Begin the exercise. (Remind the participants that even though the recipients are told what the object is, they are to hand it back and ask what it is.)

6. Once everyone is familiar with the procedure and the objects are about two-thirds of the way around, you may introduce an element of competition to see whose object goes around the circle first.

7. There will be a person in the group for whom the two objects cross over. This usually results in great hilarity but may need encouragement from you to the person concerned who will want to "do it right."

Trainer Guidance

Following is a suggested explanation of this exercise. "We are going to play a silly game which will be a great energizer. I know that these things look like flipchart pens [or some other object] but in fact, this is a 'ding' and this is a 'dong' [hold them up so everyone is clear which is which].

"Now I'm going to pass the 'ding' around to the right and say 'this is a ding'. Of course [*name*] will have her doubts and so she will hand it back to me asking 'what?' and I shall repeat 'ding' and pass it back to her. She will pass it on to the next person [*name*], who, also hands it back to [*name*] asking 'what?' . Since [*name*] is no longer sure what it is, passes it back to me also asking 'what.' Again I am able to reassure her saying 'ding' so she can pass it on to [*name*] confidently saying 'ding' and he will pass it on to the next person [*name*], saying 'This is a ding!' This will continue around the entire circle.

"At the same time, [*name of person on your left*] will pass the 'dong' around the other way but the same thing happens; each person has to query what it is and pass it back to the start to be reassured."

Variation

If your group don't seem to grasp the idea very quickly, you can start the "ding" going around until they seem more confident before introducing the "dong" going the other way. (The exercise will not be a competitive one, however, do it correctly).

Possible Pitfalls

On the face of it, this is merely an amusing game that deteriorates into helpless laughter, and it's up to you to stop the game. There may be some participants, however, who take the game very seriously and have a real need to do it correctly. Be sure to address the needs of these participants.

Most groups enjoy this game immensely. They have been known to ask for it to be repeated the following day.

Notes

12
Do I Trust You?

Objective

The purpose of this activity is to develop trust within a group. It is especially useful for training courses on personal development, awareness among groups or on team building.

Material

None.

Time

30 minutes.

Method

1. Ask participants to form pairs. (If you have any groups of three, you will need to allow more time.)

2. Explain to participants that they will do two exercises with each person in the pair taking a turn being the leader:

   a. the leader guides his/her partner, who has his/her eyes closed, around the room gently and slowly;

   b. the leader promises to catch his/her partner as he/she falls backward to the floor

3. Make certain that the leaders tell their partners they will be safe.

4. If anyone is not comfortable with this exercise, he/she has the option of not participating. Allow enough time for each person to take the lead and for some feedback among partners in between exercises.

5. When you come back into the group, lead a discussion about the exercise. Some questions you could ask are:

- How did that feel?
- What was it like when you were leading?
- How did your feelings change toward the other person in the second exercise?

Variation

Activity 48 may be used as an ending exercise for this same group.

Possible Pitfalls

This exercise requires commitment (and courage!) from the participants, which you should acknowledge.

It can produce feelings that need to be addressed sensitively and may lead to other exercises that build on the importance of trust in teams and groups.

Notes

13

Fruit

Objective

The purpose of this activity is to remember people's names and have some fun!

It is useful as a beginning exercise for a group that has already trained together or for an existing team, or it can be used as an energizer after lunch.

Material

None.

Time

20 minutes.

Method

1. Ask everyone to stand with you in a circle.

2. Ask participants to choose a fruit or vegetable, to tell the group what it is and then to "mime" it as creatively as they can. This is not a conventional miming game because the others are not being challenged to guess what fruit/vegetable you are. What is called for is some physical action that represents the fruit/vegetable.

3. As the trainer, you start first by saying your name and then performing (miming) your actions while saying "and I'm a . . ."

4. The next person in the circle on your right then has to introduce you and repeat your mime before doing his/her own saying: "This is . . . and she's a . . . My name's . . . and I'm a . . ."

5. As you go around the circle, each person begins with you, repeats everyone else's mime, finishing with their own.

6. Once each person has had a turn, ask the group together to go around the circle doing all the mimes one at a time beginning with yours, so that all the group act being a pineapple, lemon, mushroom, etc.

7. If, as you go around, someone cannot remember a mime, you (and the group) can gently assist by miming the fruit/vegetable. They will soon remember.

Variation

Ask the group to guess the fruit or vegetable being mimed.

Possible Pitfalls

This is an extremely silly game and some participants may be embarrassed by this type of activity, which is why it should never be used "cold" with a group. Always be prepared to model "foolish" behavior first and to gently encourage the less forthcoming to join in. It is well worth the risk involved as it creates a good rapport in the group.

Notes

14
Getting To Know You

Objective

The purpose of this activity, is for participants to start to get to know each other. It can be used to raise people's awareness of the assumptions we make about others. It is particularly useful for personal awareness training.

Materials

*   Flipchart and pen.

Time

30 minutes.

Method

1. Explain the purpose of the activity and write on the flipchart the information you want the pairs of participants to share.

2. Ask participants to move around the room and choose someone who has something in common such as hair color, who they would like to get to know.

3. Ask these pairs to exchange their names, jobs and what it feels like to have, this characteristic in common with someone they don't know.

4. After a few minutes ask the pairs to split and form a new pairing according to something else they have in common, for example, the same eye color. This pair exchanges the same information as before.

5. Continue pairing people according to what they have in common, such as the same:

- color socks
- weight
- age
- birth sign
- length of hair
- size shoes, etc.

6. If participants are pairing up with someone according to a characteristic that they may be <u>uncertain</u> about, such as age, they will have to confirm their assumptions.

7. Continue for at least four pairings.

8. Ask everyone to sit down again and lead a short review session, asking questions of the group:

- How did you enjoy the exercise?
- What did you learn?
- How did your awareness of people change as the exercise progressed?
- How accurate were you in the assumptions you made about people, (step 6) e.g. on the basis of their physical appearance? What can we learn from this?

If you are pairing up with someone according to something you don't know *for certain* that you have in common, your age for example, you will need to exchange that information too to ensure that you were right!

Variation

Once one pair has exchanged information, ask them to join with another pair who are the opposite or different, e.g. short people with tall people, green-eyed people with blue-eyed people. They then exchange names, jobs and share what it is like to be *different*.

Notes

15

Great Expectations

Objective

The purpose of this activity, suitable for any group, is for participants to introduce each other and learn each other's expectations.

Materials

Flipchart and pen.

Time

30 minutes.

Method

1. Go around the group and ask participants, one at at a time, to introduce themselves by saying their name and one expectation they have about the course.

2. Write each expectation on the flipchart. At the end of the course, refer to the list to see how to what extent these expectations have been met.

Variation

Ask for one expectation and one fear.

Notes

16

Guess Whose

Objective

The purpose of this activity, suitable for any group, is for participants to introduce each other and learn something about each other.

Materials

None that need to be provided by the trainer, but participants will need to have some items normally carried in a wallet or purse (see step 2 below).

Time

30 minutes.

Method

1. Ask participants to pair up with someone they don't already know, and to introduce themselves to each other.

2. When in their pairs each person should select two objects of their own to lend to the other person; these can be taken from a bag, pocket, wallet, off the persons themselves, and should have some significance for the person. Make sure they know these things will be returned.

3. In the large circle ask one pair to volunteer to go first and to introduce themselves to the rest of the group. One person in that pair must then tell the whole group what he/she can deduce partner with simply from the objects presented. The partner then agrees with or corrects what has been said and if desired, adds to the information. The pair then exchanges roles.

4. Go around the group until all pairs have spoken and then make sure the objects are returned to their owners.

Notes

17
Hobbies

Objective

The purpose of this activity, suitable for any group, is to learn each other's names and something about each other.

Materials

None.

Time

20 minutes.

Method

1. Ask participants to sit in a circle and then explain the purpose of this activity.

2. Ask each person to choose a hobby they enjoy doing in their spare time that they will mime for the group.

3. As the trainer, you go first, introducing yourself and then miming your hobby, which the group has to guess.

4. The next person in the circle has to introduce you and repeat your mime ("This is . . . and s/he enjoys . . .") and then his/her own name and does his/her mime.

5. As you go around the circle, each person begins with you and repeats everyone else's name and mime until everyone has had a turn.

6. If someone can't remember a mime, then you and the rest of the group can assist by miming the action. The person will soon remember.

Variation

If this seems to go quickly (or the group is small), you can go around a second time, repeating the first round mimes before the second round.

Possible Pitfalls

Some people may be embarrassed at miming in front of a group of people, so gently encourage them to do the best they can.

Notes

18

How Are You Feeling?

Objective

The purpose of this activity is for participants to get to know each other and to share some feelings about being in a group. This activity is particularly useful in awareness training.

Materials

None.

Time

15 to 20 minutes.

Method

1. Ask participants to sit in a circle.

2. Explain to participants that each person is going to introduce him-/herself and express a feeling about being in this group.

3. As the trainer, you begin by saying your name and one feeling about being in the group. Choose a feeling that is positive to give to the group confidence as they will be looking to you for support (so don't say "I'm nervous", even if it is true!).

4. Then, go around the group giving each participant the opportunity to do the same. Be sure at this point, to tell participants that they are to be candid, and if they are nervous or uncomfortable to be sure to say so.

Variations

Ask the group to do the exercise as described above and then go around again asking each participant to say a sentence in the feeling they expressed and a reason for the feeling. For example, "I am Michele and I am very nervous to be here in this group today as it is the first time that I have been in a large group."

Notes

19
I Want To Be

Objective

The purpose of this activity, suitable for any group, is to get to know each other and share some fantasies!

Materials

None.

Time

30 minutes.

Method

1. Ask the group to sit in a circle.

2. Ask participants to think of a famous person, living or dead, fictional or real, political, artistic, etc., whom they would like to be and why.

3. Go around the group giving everyone the opportunity to express him-/herself as that person.

4. Go round again asking participants, one at a time, to introduce themselves by their real names and say what it feels like to be themselves.

Notes

20
Journey To The Group

Objective

The purpose of this activity is to start the day in a relaxed manner.

Materials

None.

Time

30 minutes.

Method

1. Ask participants to sit comfortably and close their eyes.

2. Read through the instructions aloud (see Trainer Guidance) slowly and distinctly.

3. Ask people to open their eyes and take a few seconds to be fully "back" into the room.

4. Go around and ask participants, one at a time, to say their name, their symbol and what that means to them.

5. Ask the group for comments on their feelings about the exercise.

Trainer Guidance

Following is a suggested explanation of the exercise:

"Close your eyes and make yourselves comfortable. Take a deep breath and as you breathe out allow every part of your body to relax and become limp. Let me invite you to imagine that you are now leaving the place where you were this morning, wherever it was, and as you are retracing the trip, I would like you to pay attention to any interesting incidents or conversations that you had or things that you saw. You might not have had time to pay attention to these before. Allow any irritation and tension of that trip to be left behind and forgotten so you can concentrate on the interesting aspects and give your mind a chance to see it differently. Then choose an object, a word, a color or something else that symbolizes your trip in a positive way. I'll give you a few minutes to do that on your own [allow 2—3 minutes silence].

"Now it's time for you to open your eyes and come back into this room and introduce yourself by your name and the symbol of your journey and what that symbol means using just a few words."

Possible Pitfalls

Some people say they can't imagine anything or don't want to join in. Encourage them but don't force them and when you go around at the end, ask them to say their name and maybe choose a symbol that positively describes their journey. If they can't, then ask them for their name only.

Notes

21
Left Luggage

Objective

The purpose of this activity, suitable for any group, is for participants to introduce each other and think about the course they're attending.

Materials

None.

Time

30 minutes.

Method

1. Ask people to pair up, preferably with someone they don't know.

2. Give each pair 4 minutes (2 minutes each) to introduce themselves, say where they work and the preoccupations they set aside in order to attend the training course that day. (The preoccupations could be anything, such as their work responsibilities or how long it took to get ready in the morning.) Remind each person in the pair when his/her 2 minutes is up.

3. Back in the large group, ask participants, one at a time, to introduce themselves, say where they work and say one preoccupation they've left behind (if they want to).

Notes

22

Life Collage

Objective

The purpose of this activity is for participants to experience in-depth introductions of one another. This activity is particularly useful for any group that will be together for some time, either in one session, a series of sessions or any in-house course. It can be particularly useful for any program with elements of career planning in it.

Materials

- A variety of magazines that reflect a very wide range of activities, fashion, people, etc.
- One pair of scissors per person.
- One glue stick per person.
- Sheets of flipchart paper and pens.

Time

- 30 minutes to look at magazines and choose the pictures they want to use (no cutting is allowed during this time).
- 20 minutes to cut and glue pictures on flipchart paper.
- 5 minutes per person to present their collage.

Method

1. Ask each participant to take a sheet of flipchart paper, turn it on its side lengthwise and divide it into two sections, the top being "WORK" and the bottom being "OUTSIDE WORK." Then sub-divide each section into three: Past, Present and Future so that the page is now divided into six sections. (You should have an example prepared ahead of time.)

2. Explain that you want them to make a collage of their lives by cutting out pictures that represent the areas mentioned in step 1. Letters or words may also be cut out, but pictures are to be used as much as possible.

3. Your role now is to keep track of time and deal with any difficulties people may experience—though generally participants manage very happily on their own with this exercise!

4. When the entire group comes back together, ask for a volunteer to come up to the flipchart and explain her/his collage to the group. Either you or other group members can ask questions for clarification.

5. These collages can then be put up on the walls (make sure names are on them) and left there for the duration of the course.

Possible Pitfalls

As this is a highly personal exercise, it *could* generate some intense feelings for group members. You need to remain alert to this.

Notes

23

Messages From My Past

Objective

The purpose of this activity is to get to know each other. It is particularly useful for awareness training.

Materials

None.

Time

20 minutes.

Method

1. Ask participants to think of a phrase, positive or negative, that they can still remember from their past. This can be a phrase used by a parent, teacher or anyone who was significant to them.

2. Ask the group to mill around and when they meet someone else to say their name and tell them their "phrase", e.g. "My name is Elizabeth and I must tidy my room!"

3. They repeat the same message to each person they meet.

4. Continue until all the participants have introduced themselves to each other.

5. Take general feedback about how that felt and what they think of those messages now they are adults.

Notes

24

My Fantasy

Objective

The purpose of this activity, suitable for any group, is for participants to introduce each other.

Materials

None.

Time

20 minutes.

Method

1. Ask participants to pair up with someone they don't know.

2. Ask them to introduce themselves to each other and discuss any fantasies they have in life or anything they have always wanted to do or achieve.

3. Bring them back to the large group after about 10 minutes and ask each person to introduce him-/herself and tell one fantasy to the rest of the group.

Notes

25

My Secret Self

Objective

The purpose of this activity is to encourage participants to open up and share something about themselves at the beginning of a course. (Participants can decide how personal they wish to be.)

Materials

None.

Time

5 minutes.

Method

1. Ask everyone to sit in a circle.

2. Explain that you would like participants, one at a time, to state their names, and to tell something about themselves, such as a hobby or a pet.

Some examples are:

- My name is . . . and I have two cats.
- My name is . . . and I learn tap dancing.

3. Begin the activity by taking the first turn.

Possible Pitfalls

1. Some people feel what they have to say is not as interesting or valid as others in the group so each person needs encouragement by the trainer.

Occasionally, someone <u>may</u> reveal something very personal, which needs to be treated sensitively.

Notes

26
Obituary

Objective

The purpose of this activity is for participants to gain insight into the way people perceive themselves. This activity is particularly suitable for training on personal development with any group but is more acceptable for personal development groups.

Materials

None.

Time

30 minutes.

Method

1. Ask participants to sit in a circle.

2. Instruct participants to imagine they are writing their own obituary. Have them think of three positive attributes for which they would like to be remembered, either personal qualities or accomplishments. These do not have to be profound.

3. Go around the circle, and have each participant individually give his/her name and the three remarks.

Possible Pitfalls

People may make various types of remarks so you need to be sensitive and supportive of everyone's experience.

Notes

27

Personal Shield

Objective

The purpose of this activity is for participants to introduce, and learn more about, each other. It is particularly suitable for any group who will be together in an extended program, a series of programs, or in an in-house course.

Material

- Sufficient sheets of flipchart paper for each participant.
- Flipchart pens.
- Some type of adhesive tape.

Time

45 minutes.

Method

1. Prepare ahead of time an outline of a shield drawn on flipchart paper, inside the shield, write the questions you wish to ask the participants.

2. Ask each participant to take a sheet of flipchart paper and a pen and draw a shield.

3. Within the shield ask them to draw or write the following:

- symbol that represents them (to be drawn in the center of the shield);
- a significant date
- the name of an organization that has been important to them
- the name of a person who has been/is important to them
- one quality they are proud to possess
- one expectation of the course
- anything additional that relates to the topic (see Variations).

4. Allow about 20 minutes and then ask each person to explain his/her shield to the rest of the group.

5. The shield can be put up on the walls and remain there until the end of the training and then participants can be encouraged to take them home.

Variations

This shield format can be adapted to suit any training course and the elements included can be more or less personal depending on the group and the topic. You can also ask specific questions, e.g. about management: ask for an example of a good manager or an example of ineffective management you have experienced.

Notes

28
Picture of Myself

Objective

The purpose of this activity is for participants to introduce (or re-introduce) each other and for the trainer to get an idea of how individual participants see themselves.

This activity is particularly useful for ongoing groups.

Materials

- A sheet of flipchart paper for each participant.
- Colored flipchart pens, at least one per person.

Time

20 minutes to "draw" and 3 minutes each for introductions.

Method

1. Ask participants to take a sheet of paper and a pen(s).

2. Explain that as their (re)introduction to the group, you want them to draw a picture of how they see themselves at the moment. If this is an on going group, suggest that participants reflect on how they felt at the end of the last session and how they feel now before deciding what to draw.

3. Reassure them that good drawing skills are not necessary for this and that the picture can be as diagrammatic as they choose.

4. The picture can be a full-length drawing, the head and shoulders or just the face, whatever they feel they want and can include other people or situations. They can even add thought "bubbles" containing key words coming out of their heads or mouths. Tell them also to add their name to the drawing.

5. Tell them they have about 20 minutes for the drawing. It sometimes takes people quite awhile to start. If after about 5 minutes someone seems to be having difficulty, gently find out what the problem is and offer encouragement.

6. When everyone has finished, ask each person, in turn, to bring his/her drawing to the flipchart and explain it.

7. The pictures can be displayed on the wall for the remainder of the course and at the end participants may take them home.

Variation

Ask participants to draw a picture only of themselves, without words and, without anyone or anything else. This approach does not allow them to show themselves in relation to others.

Possible Pitfalls

You need to be sensitive to what people put in their pictures and how they depict themselves. This can reveal a great deal about how people see themselves in relation to others in their lives. It can also produce some disturbing feelings for participants, which need careful treatment.

Notes

29

Reincarnation

Objective

The purpose of this activity, suitable for any group, is for participants to introduce each other and to learn something about each other.

Materials

None.

Time

15 to 20 minutes.

Method

1. Ask participants to sit in a circle.

2. Ask them to think for a few minutes about what person, animal or object they would like to come back as if they were reincarnated, and why.

3. Ask for someone to volunteer or choose someone and ask that person to say his/her name first and then who or what they would like to be reincarnated as and why.

4. Go around until everyone has had a chance to speak.

Variation

Participants could choose famous characters from history or literature.

Notes

30
Shaking Out

Objective

The purpose of this activity, suitable for any group, is to provide participants with a warm-up and an energizer.

Materials

None.

Time

20 minutes.

Method

1. Ask everyone to stand in a circle and give themselves plenty of space.

2. Start by asking them to shake their hands up and down in a brisk manner, keeping their hands next to their body. You should demonstrate this and do it with them.

3. Continue for a few seconds and then expand this movement by throwing out the arm from the shoulder with an open hand in a rhythmic movement.

4. Add to this by kicking one leg out from the hip on the same side as the arm movement.

5. Ask each member to add some noise to this, e.g. grunting, shouting, whistling.

6. Ask them to stop making the noise and then start again on the other side of the body with the hand, then shoulder, then leg, then adding the noise.

Notes

31

Shapes

Objective

The purpose of this activity is for participants to introduce and learn something about each other. This activity is particularly useful in personal development courses.

Materials

- Sheets of colored construction paper (six colors).
- Scissors.
- Templates for shapes, e.g. star, circle, square, triangle, oval, rectangle.

Time

30 minutes.

Method

1. Cut the construction paper into a variety of abstract shapes in different colors so that you have at least twice as many shapes as there are people in the group. Each shape should be about the size of a hand.

2. Put the shapes in a pile in the center of the floor in front of the participants and ask each member of the group to look at the pieces of paper, handle them and select one of a color and shape that appeals to them.

3. When each person has chosen, ask the participants, one at a time, to introduce themselves and say why they chose that particular shape and color: in other words explain the significance of their choice ("red is my favorite color; my car is red; I feel like a star," etc.). As this is a rather abstract exercise and it relies on people's interpretation of shapes and colors, it is impossible to predict what might happen. However, this is part of the strength of the event.

Variations

You could use cards with particular shapes, e.g. cat, car, sailing boat, although this would change the abstract nature of the exercise.

Notes

32

Snapshot

Objective

The purpose of this activity is for participants to share information about each other, to be aware of the "baggage" each person brings to a course (this can be useful information for the trainer also!) and, to provide continuity with an "Ending" exercise (See activity 64.) This activity is particularly useful for those attending a course that is three days or longer, is part of an ongoing program or involves personal development activities.

Materials

- 8 1/2" x 11"envelopes for each person.
- Selection of colored felt pens — at least one per person.
- Some type of adhesive tape.

Time

20 minutes to "draw" and approximately 3 minutes each for introductions.

Method

1. Ask participants to take an envelope and a pen(s).

2. Ask them to imagine that someone is taking a snapshot of them at this moment that will show how they feel, what the concerns and preoccupation's are in their lives, etc.

3. Ask each person to write their name and draw this snapshot on the *front* of their envelope, using the envelope lengthwise with the flap at the top (this is important if you are to use this envelope again in an Ending activity).

4. Explain that they can use diagrams, pictures, symbols and a few words but the emphasis is on some form of pictorial representation of how they feel now.

5. Reassure people that good drawing skills are not required for this and that everyone will be asked to explain their "photographs" to the rest of the group at the end.

6. Tell them they have about 20 minutes to draw and have them begin the exercise. It sometimes takes people quite awhile to start. If, after about 5 minutes, someone seems to be having difficulty, gently find out what the problem is and encourage them to try.

7. As people finish, ask them to stick their snapshots on the wall so that they are all displayed.

8. As a group, cluster around the display and ask for a volunteer to introduce him-/herself to the group by explaining his/her snapshot. After the explanation, other members can ask questions about the snapshot for clarification.

9. Someone else elects to go next and so on until all participants have had an opportunity to explain their snapshots.

10. Leave these envelopes on the wall until the end of the day, or ideally, until the end of the course if you are using them as an ending activity.

Variations

1. You could join in, if you feel this is appropriate, and do your own snapshot. This is necessary if you are also using this as an Ending activity and you want to receive positive messages from the group yourself (See activity 64).

2. This activity could be used purely as a "beginning" in which case a sheet of 8 1/2" x 11" paper can be used for each participant instead of an envelope.

Possible Pitfalls

You can never predict what "baggage" people bring with them to courses and this exercise could arouse all types feelings in group members as they remember their concerns and preoccupation's. You therefore need to remain sensitive to this.

Notes

33

Success Story

Objective

The purpose of this activity is for participants to recognize the successes in their lives. This activity is particularly useful for any group working on personal development issues whose past experience may have been negative.

Materials

None.

Time

Allow 3 minutes per person.

Method

1. Make sure you have a contract of confidentiality and support within the group.

2. Ask people to sit in a circle quite close together.

3. Explain that you want them to think about the success in their lives and the ways in which they have triumphed, perhaps under very difficult circumstances. Go around the group asking for a volunteer to start, allowing everyone 3 minutes. If anyone should focus on a negative experience, remind them that they are reviewing their triumphs and successes.

4. Be sure to tell participants that their successes may be from the past or present, whatever they choose.

5. Observe the time limit quite strictly. Most people find 3 minutes a very long time and will need to be encouraged to keep going. Even if someone says he/she finished, allow them the full time as they may well need that time

for thinking or speaking further. If someone is still speaking after 3 minutes, gently interrupt them as it is unfair for someone to dominate and take more time than others. Issues may be raised that will be mentioned later in the course.

6. Model attentive listening in the way *you* listen to each person; don't allow others to interrupt.

Variation

If the group members find it particularly difficult to begin, you might want to take the first turn, but be careful not to intimidate the group with your experiences as you may have had many more advantages, e.g. education, social, than they have.

Possible Pitfalls

An exercise as personal as this can raise many issues and you have to be prepared and able to treat these sensitively. Be sure to give each person that is speaking your complete attention and respect and encourage them to use the allocated time by prompting with questions such as "Is there anything elso you would like to tell us about your successes?"

Notes

34
Suitcases

Objective

The purpose of this activity, suitable for any group, is for participants to learn people's names (first names only).

Materials

None.

Time

15 to 20 minutes.

Method

1. Ask participants to sit in a circle.

2. Explain that you want each person to think of taking a vacation and packing a suitcase. Ask them to think of something they would take on vacation that they would pack.

3. As the trainer, you start first and say "My name is . . . and when I went on vacation I packed in my suitcase a . . ."

4. The person on your right goes next beginning with you, stating your name and what you said and then his/her own name, i.e. "This is . . . and when she went on her vacation she packed in her suitcase a . . . ; My name's . . . and when I went on vacation I packed a . . . in my suitcase."

5. Then the next person begins with you, followed by the person on his/her left who just had a turn and so on, until you reach the last person, who has to remember the names of the entire group and what each packed.

Notes

35
Three Faces of Me

Objective

The purpose of this activity is for participants to get to know, and share feelings about each other. It is particularly suited for awareness training.

Materials

None.

Time

30 minutes.

Method

1. Decide whether or not you will join in, remembering that it helps participants to feel less self-conscious if you do.

2. Ask each person to think about three personal characteristics that they are willing to mime to the group.

3. Ask everyone to stand up in a circle.

4. You start first (if you are joining in). Move into the center of the group, say your name and mime one of your characteristics, e.g. "My name is Harinder and I'm joyful" (jumping up and down). Then go back to your place, think for a second and come back into the center to show your second characteristic and then do the same for the third.

5. Ask for a volunteer to go next who does the same thing, e.g. "My name is Winston and I'm caring" (miming embracing), and so on until he has mimed his three faces.

6. Go around the group until everyone has completed a turn.

Possible Pitfalls

People may need coaxing and encouraging to take part but the effort is worthwhile.

Notes

36
Travel Agents

Objective

The purpose of this activity, suitable for any group, is for participants to learn people's names (first names only).

Materials

None.

Time

15 to 20 minutes.

Method

1. Ask participants to sit in a circle.

2. Explain that you want them to think of a place they would like to visit. Each person thinks of a place that begins with the same letter or has the same sound as their first name (e.g. Winston/Wyoming, Kate/California, Baljinder/Boston).

3. As the trainer you start first saying "My name is ... and I've just been to the travel agent to book a trip to ..."

4. The person on your right goes next beginning with your name and destination and then his/her own, "this is ... and she's booked a trip to ... And my name's ... and I've booked a trip to ..."

5. The next person again begins with you, followed by the person on his/her left who just had a turn and so on, until you reach the last person who has to remember the names and destinations of the entire group.

Notes

37
Where Do I Fit In?

Objective

The purpose of this activity is for participants to express nonverbally their perceived position in relation to the group itself and in relation to each other. This activity is particularly useful for personal awareness training or in an ongoing group.

Materials

Something large enough to be a focal point for the group, e.g. a basket or a bin.

Time

30 minutes.

Method

1. Choose the object you want to use to represent the group and place it in the center of the room.

2. Ask participants to join in (see Trainer Guidance) and allow them time to alter their position if they want to.

3. Reposition the large group and ask people how they are feeling and what they learned from this exercise or any other comment they want to make.

Trainer's Guidance

The following suggested introduction may be used to explain the activity: "I am going to put this object in the center of the room so that it is symbolic of the center of this group.

"I shall then ask one of you to volunteer and take a position as close to the center or as far away from the center of this group depending on how you feel at the moment in relation to the group. Also, show how you feel, e.g. embracing the group with arms outstretched, feeling small by crouching down, and so on — whatever feeling you want to express physically. You are not to *say* anything!

"Another person will then be asked to volunteer to take a position not only in relation to the center of the group but also in relation to the person who is already there and also to express physically how she/he feels.

"When everyone is placed in the group I shall ask each one of you to be aware of your position in relation to the center of the group and to every other member of the group and also the physical position you have adopted. If you then want to change position closer to the center, for example, you may do so.

"Think about what it feels like to be in a new position and then we'll come back together in the group."

Possible Pitfalls

You need to be sensitive to the positions people find themselves in, as they may feel very isolated or rejected. Allow time to process any feelings that come up before moving on.

Notes

38
Where in the World?

Objective

The purpose of this activity, suitable for any group, is for participants to introduce participants, and learn more about each other.

Materials

- A large outline map of the world.
- Self-sticking removable notes—two per person.
- Pens.

Time

30 minutes.

Method

1. Attach the map to a wall or whiteboard at the front of the room.

2. Ask each participant to take two pieces of paper and a pen.

3. Each person should think quietly of two places in the world that are of particular significance to them and to write down the names of those places. These places can be countries, cities, or even street names.

4. Ask participants, individually, to come to the front and introduce themselves and stick their papers on the corresponding place on the map explaining why these places are important. (If a participant is not sure where his/her choices are located on the map, everyone may help out.)

Variations

1. If you have a large group or not much time, the activity can be limited to one choice.

2. You could just use a U.S. map and ask people to be very specific about their choices, giving exact addresses. However, remember that not all participants may have been born in the United States, so try to determine that from your participant group.

Notes

39

Who Cleaned Their Teeth This Morning?

Objective

The purpose of this lighthearted activity is for participants to form groups and learn something about each other. This activity is particularly useful with a group that knows each other somewhat or with an existing team.

Materials

A chair for each person.

Time

15 to 20 minutes.

Method

1. Arrange enough chairs for each participant in a long line facing the front.

2. Ask everyone to sit down.

3. Ask people to change chairs according to your instructions given in step 6. Start with several instructions that you know people will have to respond to and move then follow with more varied instructions. You may add anything you can think of to vary the list below.

4. Watch how people are moving so that you can choose instructions that vary the number of seats people move. It's fun to end up with four or five people sitting on the same chair!

5. Conclude the activity when you judge people have had enough.

6. Following are the instructions you will give:

- If you brushed your teeth this morning, move three seats to the left.
- If you read a newspaper regularly, move one seat to the right.
- If you have been on vacation this year, move four seats to the left.
- If you like to be outdoors, move one seat to the left.
- If you like Chinese food, move, etc.
- If you eat chocolate, move, etc.
- If you are good at practical things, move, etc.
- If you wear glasses, move, etc.
- If you enjoy gardening, move, etc.
- If you traveled overseas last year, move, etc.
- If you like eating in restaurants, move, etc.
- If you enjoy working for . . . [name of the organization], move, etc.
- If you are good at being a manager [if appropriate], move, etc.
- If you like animals, move, etc.

Possible Pitfalls

1. Be aware of the physical condition of participants (disability, pregnancy, size, etc.) and *only* use this activity if you feel participants will not be harmed or unduly embarrassed.

2. Be sensitive to gender and cultural norms relating to physical closeness.

Notes

40
Zodiac Game

Objective

The purpose of this activity, suitable for any group, is for participants to introduce each other and discover each other's expectations of the course.

Materials

- Twelve sheets of paper, each with a different sign of the zodiac together with the dates for each birth sign.
- Flipchart paper and pens.
- Some type of adhesive tape.

Time

45 minutes.

Method

1. Post your zodiac sheets around the walls of the training room, spreading them out as much as possible. Choose the questions that you want them to discuss and write them on the flipchart. Do not reveal them yet.

2. Ask each person to go and stand under the sheet that represents their birth sign. Be sure to tell participants that this is *not* about believing in horoscopes.

3. Explain that you want them to form groups with those of the same birth sign (groups of 3 to 5). If you don't have enough for any one sign then put two or three smaller groups together, as far as possible from "adjoining" star signs.

4. Give a piece of flipchart paper to each group. Ask them to introduce themselves to each other and discuss these questions: what they have in common apart from their sign of the zodiac, any significant differences between them and how they as a group expect to benefit from the training. If you have people with different birth signs together, ask them to discuss what is different about them, any significant commonalties and what they expect to gain from the course. Ask them to record the main points of their discussion on flipchart paper and choose a spokesperson to provide the feedback.

5. After about 20 minutes ask the spokesperson from each group to come to the flipchart, introduce each member of her/his group and provide feedback of what they discussed.

6. When each group has spoken you may wish to pick up on their expectations and clarify the aims and objectives of the course.

Variations

1. You can use this as a way of randomly dividing the group for any activity.

2. You can choose any questions you wish once they are in their groups.

Notes

PART TWO:
Endings

We often use some form of exercise to begin a training event because we know the benefits to the rest of the course. When the training program draws to a close, however, often no specific "ending" exercise is used. Participants may be given an evaluation form to fill in and that is all.

Endings are equally necessary to provide closure and recognize the conclusion of any experience, before moving on, and it validates what has been shared over the period of the course. Ending exercises don't need to be deep and meaningful; often they can be fun, but you may well find, with a group that has worked together over a long period of time and has grown together, that some endings can be quite emotional.

Providing a means of formally saying "goodbye" to the group is the main reason for ending activities. Other reasons include:

1. Providing a shared experience for the group before closing;

2. Allowing participants to recognize what they have gained from the course and think about how to apply their learning;

3. Evaluating the course;

4. Seeing if expectations have been met;

5. Providing feedback for the trainer.

41
Action!

Objective

The purpose of this activity, suitable for any group, is to encourage participants to make action plans and be committed to carrying them out.

Materials

Paper and pens.

Time

30 minutes.

Method

1. Ask each participant to reflect on what they have gained from the course and what they are going to do as a result of it by dividing a sheet of paper into three columns labeled "Six months," "Three months" and "Tomorrow!" and complete each column.

2. Reassure participants that its not always possible to make instant changes and, in fact, it's easier to think in the long term about action plan objectives. Participants may like to begin with what they want to achieve in six months' time and then work back until they come to a list of what they are going to do tomorrow.

3. Allow about 15 minutes for this and then come back into the large group and ask each person to read aloud one significant item from each column.

Variation

If you have a follow-up session or work with this group again, you could write up the significant plans that are offered and circulate them to the members of the group so that you can refer to them when you meet again. Make sure participants are clear about what you are going to do and reassure people that if they haven't achieved it by the next meeting then they should still come back. Far from intimidating people, this method helps to reinforce the commitment to action.

Notes

42

And Now "Goodbye"

Objective

The purpose of this activity is for participants to formally acknowledge the ending of the training. It is particularly suited for ongoing groups.

Materials

None.

Time

30 minutes.

Method

1. Ask participants to sit in a circle and explain that this exercise is a way to formally and literally say "goodbye," thereby *not* avoiding separation.

2. Start by demonstrating it and go around saying "goodbye" to the group as a whole and then saying "goodbye" to each member of the group, always using the word "goodbye" and the person's name.

3. Ask someone to volunteer to go next and keep going until all participants have spoken.

Notes

43

Card To Remember Me By

Objective

The purpose of this activity, suitable for any group, is for participants to leave with a positive message.

Materials

Flipchart paper or 8 1/2" x 11"colored construction paper and colored pens.

Time

30 minutes.

Method

1. Divide the group into groups of two or three. Distribute paper and pens.

2. Ask these small groups to design a card that they would like to "send" to the entire group with a picture or symbol on the outside and a message on the inside, much like any greeting card that makes a special occasion. This occasion marks the ending of the group's time together.

3. After about 20 minutes, ask each small group to present their card to the group and to explain it.

Variation

Ask each person to design a card individually.

Notes

44

Closing Circles

Objective

The purpose of this activity, suitable for any group, is to provide something that marks the conclusion of the training course and can provide some feedback for the trainer.

Materials

Flipchart and pen.

Time

30 minutes.

Method

1. Ask participants to sit in a circle.

2. Ask each participant to review the course and provide answers to these three statements:

   - One thing I've learned from the course;
   - One thing I've enjoyed;
   - One thing I would've liked more of.

   Write these on the flipchart to remind everyone.

3. Ask for a volunteer to start or choose someone and then go around so that everyone has an opportunity to answer.

Variations

There are many combinations of statements that can be used, for example:

1. What I have gained from the course? what I am going to do as a result of it?

2. One thing I have learned about myself; one important piece of feedback I received about myself.

3. One thing that surprised me about the course; one thing I'm looking forward to (this can be work or home).

Possible Pitfalls

1. Try to keep comments short while allowing each person to contribute. Don't allow anyone to use this as a chance to dominate.

2. Don't be too defensive if you hear criticism of the program. The end of a course is not the time to enter into a lengthy dialogue.

Notes

45
Color This Group

Objective

The purpose of this activity is for participants to leave the training course with positive messages. This activity is particularly suitable for any group but preferably one that has been together for some time.

Materials

Flipchart paper.

Time

30 minutes.

Method

1. Prepare a list of items that this group "could be", e.g. "if this group were a color, it would be . . ." or "if this group were a car, it would be . . ." The description should be a positive one.

Other items could include a/an:

- piece of furniture
- piece of music
- book
- flower
- article of clothing
- shape
- television program
- meal
- country
- place to live
- job
- organization
- holiday destination
- animal.

2.Write this list on flipchart paper making sure you have at least one item per participant and one for yourself if you are joining in.

3. Ask everyone to sit in a circle and ask each person, in turn, to choose an item and tell the group what they think it would be and why. You may need to demonstrate this activity. For example, if you picked "a place to live," you might say "If this group were a place to live it would be a wonderful home with many different rooms and each with much to offer."

Notes

46
Compliments

Objective

The purpose of this activity is for participants to practice giving and receiving compliments and thereby leave the training feeling good about themselves. This activity is particularly suitable for any group, but it is especially useful for assertiveness training and other confidence building and personal development courses.

Materials

None.

Time

30 minutes.

Method

1. Ask participants to sit in a circle quite close together.

2. Explain that it can be quite difficult for some to give and receive compliments but that it's beneficial to try.

3. As the trainer you start and turn to the person on your right and, using that person's first name, give him/her a compliment. You need to model confident and unembarrassed behavior. You might want to say something you have noticed about them that you admire, such as a helpful quality. (Do not focus on outward appearance.)

4. That person then accepts the compliment, assertively saying "Thank you" or something similar.

5. Go around the circle with participants giving a compliment to the person on their right until it comes back to you.

Possible Pitfalls

If you know there are two people sitting next to each other who may find this difficult, then reverse the direction of the compliments. You can usually find a way of making this slightly easier.

Notes

47

Different Ways To Say Goodbye

Objective

The purpose of this activity is to physically demonstrate "goodbye." This activity is particularly suitable for a group that has been together for some time.

Materials

None.

Time

30 minutes.

Method

1. Ask the group to think of all the ways people in different cultures say "goodbye": shaking hands, bowing, kissing both cheeks, hugging, etc.

2. Ask participants to mix with the others so that when they meet someone they use a physical means of saying goodbye.

3. They then move to another person and use another means of saying goodbye so that they go around the entire group using at least three different methods.

Variation

You may want to join in this yourself.

Possible Pitfalls

Don't use this with a group that will find this threatening because of the physical aspect. You don't want them to go away feeling uncomfortable. Remind participants to choose a method that will be comfortable for both the person saying goodbye and the recipient.

Notes

48

Do I Trust You Now? *

Objective

The purpose of this activity is for participants to demonstrate the development of trust in the group.

Materials

None.

Time

30 minutes.

Method

1. Ask the group to form the same pairs they were in at the beginning when doing Activity 12.

2. Ask them to repeat the exercises they did at the beginning of the course using this activity.

3. As a large group lead a discussion on how they now feel and if there are any differences that have emerged since doing those exercises earlier.

* This activity should be used only with groups who have used Activity 12 as a beginning exercise.

Possible Pitfalls

1. Only use this if you feel the group has developed more trust in each other during the course, otherwise you may promote a sense of failure among the group or individuals in that group.

2. Only use it if everyone joined in the first time or be prepared to use an additional ending exercise where everyone can join in.

Notes

49

Gallery of Wants and Offers

Objective

The purpose of this activity, suitable for any group, is to provide participants with an opportunity to offer a skill or some type of support to one another, as well as to ask for help or whatever they need.

Materials

- Flipchart and pens.
- Some type of adhesive tape.

Time

30 minutes.

Method

1. Give participants each a piece of flipchart paper and a pen and ask them to divide the paper into two columns, with one headed "wants" and the other headed "offers" and ask them to write down their name and telephone number (home or office, whichever they prefer).

2. Explain to participants that they are to think about what they can offer to other group members in terms of skill, information or support and what they would like to ask for that would help them further, even after the training ends. Give them 10 minutes to complete the sheets and then post them on the wall.

3. Allow 20 minutes for everyone to look around to see what people have written and then seek out the person(s) they can help or who can help them and negotiate a way to accept or give what is needed.

4. Ask participants to sit down and formally thank the group and say "goodbye".

Notes

50
Gift to the Group

Objective

The purpose of this activity is to leave the group with positive messages from each member. This activity is particularly useful for a group that has met, in increments, over a period of several months, for a week-long program or on an in-house course.

Materials

None.

Time

20 minutes.

Method

1. Ask participants to form a circle with their chairs so that they are close together.

2. Explain what you want them to do (see Trainer's Guidance) and give an example of the type of "gift" you mean.

3. When everyone is ready, you go first with your "gift" (which ensures everyone has the right idea) and then each person takes turns giving his/her gift.

Trainer Guidance

The following suggested explanation may be used to introduce the activity. As a way of saying good-bye, think of a gift you would like to give to this group. Spend about half a minute visualizing this gift, which might be a physical object, such as a boquet of flowers, or a thought or feeling, such as self-confidence—something you would like to leave with the group as a special gift from you.

"I will begin and then we'll go around so everyone will have a turn."

Variations

1. Ask participants to mime their gift as if they were sculpting it out of clay. This means the gift is physical or describes a thought or feeling.

2. Ask the group to draw or paint the gift. This will take much longer since more time will need to be allowed for the activity.

Notes

51
Group Shield

Objective

The purpose of this activity is for participants to reflect on the training course as a group and offer feedback on some aspects of the training and to to provide positive messages for the group as a whole. This activity is particularly suitable for groups that have been working together for some time.

Materials

Sheets of flipchart paper and pens.

Time

30 minutes.

Method

1. Ahead of time, draw a shield on flipchart paper divided into four with the quadrants labeled as follows:

   • Most useful aspect of the course;
   • Least useful aspect of the course;
   • A message to participants;
   • A message to the tutor(s);

Beneath the shield draw a banner where the group motto will go. The motto can be a single word or phrase. This will act as an example for the groups and explain to the participants that completing the four quadrants and creating a motto that represents the group, is the activity.

2. Divide the group into smaller groups (about three or four people in each) and ask them to complete the activity as a group.

3. After about 20 minutes ask each group to present their shield to the rest of the group.

Notes

52

Group Sound

Objective

The purpose of this activity, suitable for any group, is to have participants say "goodbye" symbolically and have fun!

Materials

None.

Time

30 minutes.

Method

1. Ask the entire group to invent a group sound. It can be a tune, a song, a sound, or even a dance. Allow 15 minutes for preparation.

2. Ask them to demonstrate it for you as a "goodbye" message.

Variations

1. Do group sculpting (see Activity 37) to see how people feel now.

2. Do group building. If you are holding the course in an area that has easy access outside you could suggest that each person go out and collect an object. The group as a whole then constructs something that symbolizes the group and presents that to you.

Notes

53

How Do I Feel Now?

Objective

The purpose of this activity is to review changes that have occured since the beginning of the course. This activity is particularly suited to personal-development training, preferably a personal development group.

Materials

Flipchart paper and colored pens.

Time

30 minutes.

Method

1. Distribute the flipchart paper and pens. Ask each person to draw a picture of how they are feeling now at the end of the course. Symbols or diagrams may be used in addition to drawing. Allow 15 minutes.

2. Give participants, one at a time, time to explain their drawing to the rest of the group.

3. As with all visual expressions, all types of feelings can emerge and especially at the end of the group session you will need to be sensitive to the apprehension some people may experience. You should allow a little time right at the end to make sure the group ends on a positive note.

Notes

54

Import-Export Game

Objective

The purpose of this activity, suitable for any group, is for participants to reflect on the training course and what they have learned from it.

Materials

Paper and pens.

Time

20 minutes.

Method

1. Explain the purpose of this activity. Explain that training may be viewed as a series of "imports" (what participants have gained) and "exports" (what participants have contributed). Emphasize that everyone contributed so, hopefully, everyone gained.

2. Ask participants to reflect on what *they* have exported and imported during the course by listing them in two columns on a sheet of paper. Give them 5 minutes to do this.

3. Give everyone the chance to say one import and one export from their list.

Notes

55

Letter to Myself

Objective

The purpose of this activity, suitable for any group, is for participants to develop action plans and to provide a mechanism to remind them of those plans after the course ends.

Materials

Paper, pens, envelopes and postage stamps.

Time

30 minutes.

Method

1. Ask participants to write a letter to themselves stating the important aspects of the course and what they intend to do as a result of the course.

2. Ask them to address an envelope to themselves either to their home or work address and seal their letter in it so that it remains confidential.

3. Explain that you will arrange to mail these letters to them in 3 months' time.

4. Assure them that you will not forget to mail the letters!

Variations

1. Mailing the letters either before or after 3 month's time may be adjusted as appropriate, depending on the training objectives.

2. Ask participants to leave the envelopes unsealed so you may add a note of encouragement when you send the letter. (Step 2 in the Method section will obviously be adapted in this variation.)

Notes

56
Letting Go

Objective

The purpose of this activity, suitable for any group, is to have participants feeling very relaxed before leaving the training session.

Materials

None.

Time

15 minutes.

Method

1. Ask participants to close their eyes and make themselves comfortable.

2. Read the instructions (see Trainer Guidance).

3. When they open their eyes, make sure they are wide awake and say "goodbye" before they go.

Trainer Guidance

The following suggested instructions may be used: "I'd like you to take a deep breath in and out gently ... and again .... Now as you breathe in, raise your shoulders right up to your ears as high as you can and hold them there for a second or two, then as you breathe out drop your shoulders suddenly and forcefully so they are right down and relaxed. Now do that again . . . and again for the last time and as you bring your shoulders down, imagine a color that is soothing or a sound that is calming or a sensation that you enjoy. Stay like that for a few seconds, then open your eyes and feel wonderful."

Notes

57
Messages in the Shoe

Objective

The purpose of this activity is to conclude the training with positive messages for all of the participants. This activity is particularly useful for a group that has been together for a while.

Material

Paper and pens.

Time

30 minutes.

Method

1. Decide whether you want to join in this activity yourself. If you do, it will enable you to give individual positive messages to group members, which can be very beneficial. You will also receive some positive messages about yourself.

2. Ask each group member to take off one of their shoes and explain the activity as follows: As a way of saying "goodbye," each person in the group will write a positive message to everyone else. This message will be about a particular quality they admire or something they learned.

3. Make sure that everyone has a sheet of paper that they can tear into pieces so that they have enough to write a message for everyone in the group and allow about 20 minutes for them to do this.

4. As they finish their messages to others, they can place this message in the shoe of the relevant person. (Participants are encouraged to sign their messages.)

5. Once all messages have been written and "delivered" allow participants time to read and absorb their messages.

6. Ask each person to select one which is especially significant to them and to read it aloud to the rest of the group without saying who it came from.

Notes

58

My, How I've Changed!

Objective

The purpose of this activity is for participants to acknowledge each person's development, and to give positive feedback to the group.

Materials

None.

Time

20 to 30 minutes.

Method

1. Ask participants to sit in a circle.

2. Ask for a volunteer to go first and say how he/she has changed or developed as a result of being in the group.

3. Go around the circle so that everyone makes a contribution.

Notes

59

My Message to You

Objectives

The purpose of this activity is for participants to give useful feedback to each other. This activity is particularly useful for an ongoing group or with awareness training.

Materials

None.

Time

30 to 40 minutes (allow 5 minutes each).

Method

1. Decide whether you want to participate in this exercise.

2. Ask the group to sit in a circle.

3. Explain the purpose of the activity.

4. Ask each participant, in turn, to go to the other members of the group and give them a message, e.g. "My message to you, Jean, is 'thank you' for your sensitivity in this group." Both giver and receiver of the message should be on the same level and therefore the giver may need to crouch down or, if this is uncomfortable, ask the receiver to stand up if he/she doesn't mind.

5. Continue until everyone has given their messages in front of the group to the others.

Notes

60

Over the Rainbow

Objective

The purpose of this activity is to acknowledge the development the group has made during training. The activity is particularly suited to a group that has been together for some time.

Materials

Flipchart paper and colored pens.

Time

30 minutes.

Method

1. Divide the group into smaller groups of three or four.

2. Give the groups flipchart paper and pens and ask them to imagine that during training the group has developed and moved on as if crossing over a rainbow. (Mention that rainbows are symbolic of hope and optimism, and you would like to view the training and development in a positive way.)

3. Ask participants to think of three goals that the group had at the start of the course and three results they have achieved from the course.

4. Write these, spaced apart, on the sheet of flipchart paper and draw a rainbow to link both together. Allow 15 minutes for this.

5. Ask each group to present their "rainbow" to the rest of the group.

Notes

61

Pairs Appreciation

Objective

The purpose of this activity, suitable for any group, is for participants to gain some positive feedback from another group member.

Materials

None.

Time

20 minutes.

Method

1. Ask participants to form pairs (or have a trio if necessary) and explain the purpose of this activity.

2. Give each person, one at at time, 5 minutes to say three things he/she likes about the other person.

3. Back in the large group ask each person to announce one of the compliments they have received, and now "own," to the rest of the group. These can be any positive attributes they've noticed about each other. Remind the pairs to assertively accept the compliments by saying "Thank you," and *not* to be embarrassed.

Notes

62

Remember Me

Objective

The purpose of this activity, suitable for any group, is to end the training on a positive note.

Materials

None.

Time

20 minutes.

Method

1. Explain the purpose of the activity.

2. Ask everyone to think of the way they would like the other group members to remember them.

3. Tell participants that this remembrance may be a specific achievement, a particular personal quality or a goal that you have set.

4. Ask each person, in turn, to announce this to the group in a confident way.

Notes

63

Review of Expectations

Objective

The purpose of this activity, suitable for any group, is to have participants evaluate the course and see if it has met their expectations.

Materials

- A list of expectations made at the beginning of the course.
- Flipchart.

Time

15 minutes.

Method

1. Explain the purpose of the activity.

2. Attach the list to the flipchart and quickly review it.

3. Looking at the list made at the beginning of the course, ask participants to what extent expectations were met. If there were shortcomings, ask what else might have been done to make the training more successful.

Possible Pitfalls

If any criticisms emerge, don't be tempted into a long discourse defending your training course.

Notes

64

Snapshot

Objective

The purpose of this activity is to make a positive connection between the beginning and ending of a training program. This activity is particularly suited to longer training programs (and that used Activity 32).

Materials

- The envelopes completed in Activity 32.
- Paper and pens.

Time

30 minutes.

Method

1. Make sure that all the envelopes are still on the wall from the beginning of the course and that they are clearly labeled with people's names.

2. Ask each participant to write a positive message to the other participants and to you if you are joining in. This activity could be about a particular quality someone has, an accomplishment, and so on.

3. As the messages are written, ask participants to place them in the relevant envelopes on the wall.

4. Make sure no one looks at their messages but takes home the envelope and reads it. Remind participants that since they have them at home to periodically look at these messages when they need encouragement and support.

5. Use some simple closing exercise (see Activity 44) or evaluation exercise to close the event formally.

Notes

65

Story Time

Objective

The purpose of this activity, suitable for any group, is to acknowledge the value of the group experience.

Materials

None.

Time

30 minutes.

Method

1. Ask people to sit in a circle. Explain the purpose of the activity.

2. Start by telling your story of the group in one sentence, for example "My name is . . . and I was in a group that brought me much joy and support and I went home feeling good about myself and positive about my future."

3. The next person then adds "And I was in the same group and that group gave me . . ." and so on around the whole group so that the story is ongoing and everyone has a chance to give feedback about the group.

Notes

66
This is Goodbye

Objective

The purpose of this activity is to symbolically and physically demonstrate "goodbye." It is particularly suited to ongoing groups or more intensive training.

Materials

A pillow or cushion or something similar that can be held or hugged.

Time

30 minutes.

Method

1. Ask participants to sit in a circle.

2. You start by taking the pillow (or suitable soft object) that symbolizes the group and addressing it by saying goodbye (and adding any comments, such as "thank you for helping me"). Participants may hug the pillow if they wish.

3. Pass on the pillow to the next person who says goodbye using the same format and his/her own words.

4. The pillow is passed round until everyone has thus addressed the group.

5. As the pillow is passed back to you at the end, announce to the group that now everyone has had a chance to say goodbye to the group the object reverts to being a pillow.

Notes

67
This Is Our Group

Objective

The purpose of this activity is for participants to appreciate the positive aspects of the training group. This activity is particularly suited to groups that have been together for some time.

Materials

Flipchart paper and pens.

Time

30 minutes.

Method

1. Divide the group into groups of three or four. Distribute paper and pens.

2. Ask each group to devise a motto or logo that, for them, sums up their feelings about the training group and write it on flipchart paper. Either words or symbols may be used. Allow about 15 minutes.

3. Come back together and ask each group to present their motto or logo and its significance to the rest of the group.

Variation

Ask the groups to devise both a logo and motto.

Notes

68

Traffic Lights

Objective

The purpose of this activity, suitable for any group, is to introduce the idea of developing an action plan at the end of a course.

Materials

- A drawing of traffic lights with red, yellow, and green lights on a piece of flipchart paper.
- Paper and pens.

Time

20 minutes.

Method

1. Put your drawing of the traffic lights on the flipchart and explain that the traffic lights represent an action plan: what participants should stop doing, what they should do less of, and what they should go forward with.

2. Ask each person to write down their own "traffic lights", using each one. Allow 5 minutes.

3. Go around the group asking each person to tell the rest of the group one of the things they will stop doing as a result of the course, one of the things they will do less of and one of the things they are going to go ahead and do.

Notes

69

What Do I Take Away with Me?

Objective

The purpose of this activity is for participants to take away positive feedback about the group. The activity is particularly suited to ongoing groups.

Materials

None.

Time

20 to 30 minutes.

Method

1. Ask participants to sit in a circle.

2. Participants, one at a time, announce their name and one quality or feeling they are taking away, e.g. "My name is Jonathan and I take with me the warmth that I felt from this group."

3. Go around the circle until everyone has had a turn.

Notes

70

You're Great as You Are, But . . .

Objective

The purpose of this activity is to give positive messages to group members and to suggest the possibility of change. This activity is particularly suited to personal-development training.

Materials

- Sheets of colored construction paper.
- Pens.

Time

30 minutes.

Method

1. Ask each participant to select a piece of paper and write their name in big letters.

2. These sheets are then placed on the floor in the center of the group and each participant picks up someone else's and writes on it "One thing I like about you" and "One thing I'd like you to change" and then signs it. Emphasize to participants that the second message should be constructively and sensitively done.

3. They return the sheet to the floor and pick up another, writing a message as before and so on until each participant has written a message on everyone else's sheet of paper.

4. Then ask participants to take back their own sheet and read aloud one of the "things I like about you" messages to the whole group.

Possible Pitfalls

Be careful about using this with a group who may have appeared to be too negative in their comments. During training suggest that any comments about changing be coached in terms of being more like, or doing more of, the positive aspects that were mentioned. You don't want people to leave feeling depressed.

Notes